Earth's Coasts

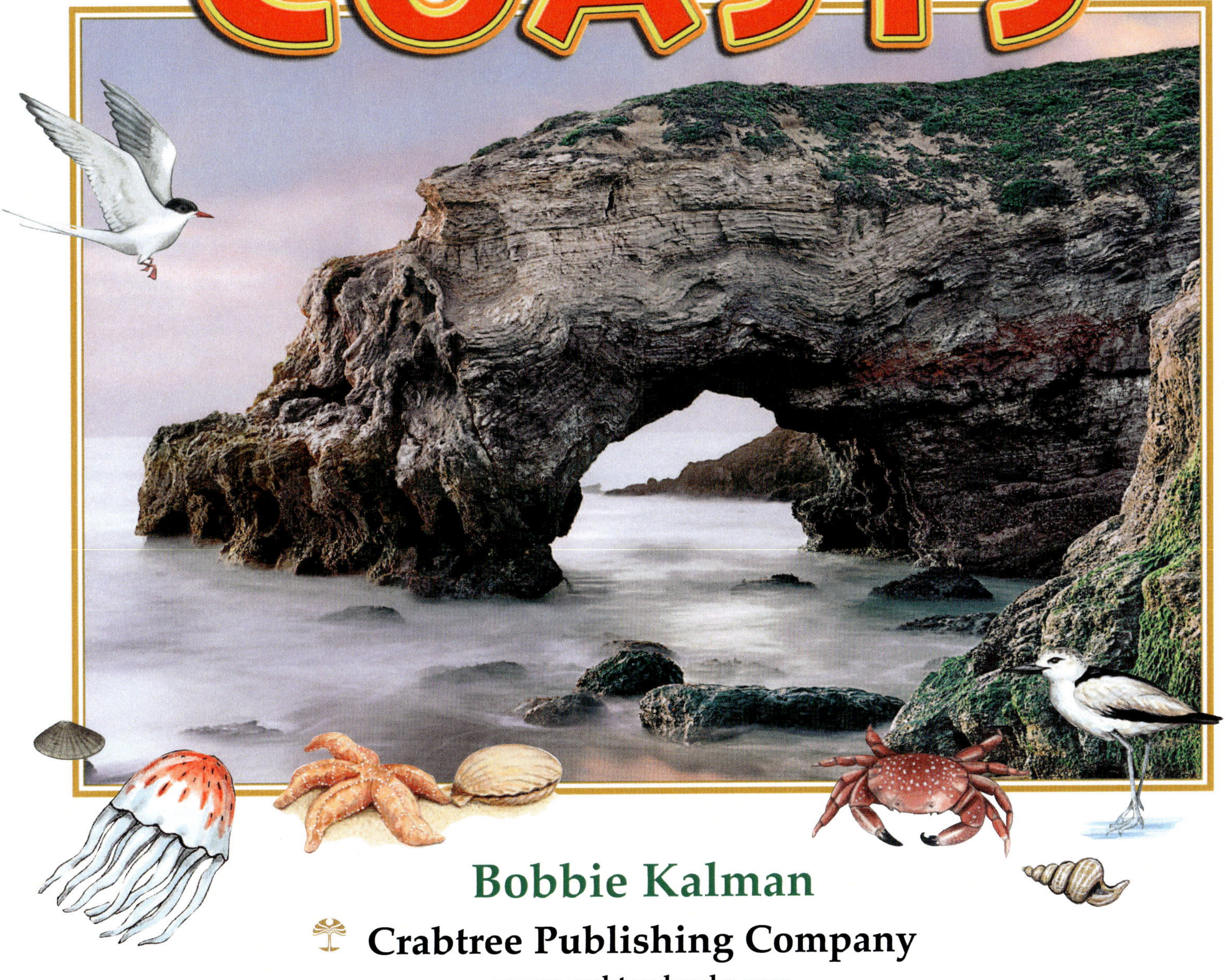

Bobbie Kalman

Crabtree Publishing Company
www.crabtreebooks.com

Created by Bobbie Kalman

For Michael Vaughan,
Happy 60th birthday! We shared some of our best times on Nassau's beautiful coasts.

Author and Editor-in-Chief
Bobbie Kalman

Editor
Kathy Middleton

Proofreader
Crystal Sikkens

Design
Bobbie Kalman
Katherine Berti
Samantha Crabtree (cover)

Production coordinator
Katherine Berti

Prepress technician
Margaret Amy Salter

Consultant
Joel Mercer,
former Head of the Geography Department,
Galt Collegiate Institute

Illustrations
Barbara Bedell: title page (jellyfish, sea star, middle shell, and right bird), pages 22 (white fish, green fish, and blue and green fish), 23 (top left and bottom left sea stars and shell), 29 (white fish and eel)
Katherine Kantor: title page (left bird, left shell, and crab), pages 5, 11, 22 (blue and black fish and yellow and blue fish), 29 (blue and black fish and skate), 30-31
Vanessa Parson-Robbs: page 23 (sea urchin)
Bonna Rouse: title page (right shell), pages 23 (top right sea star), 29 (sea star)
Margaret Amy Salter: pages 22 (yellow fish), 23 (crab), 29 (yellow fish)

Photographs
All images by Shutterstock.com except:
© Dreamstime.com: pages 25 (bottom), 27 (bottom)

Library and Archives Canada Cataloguing in Publication

Kalman, Bobbie, 1947-
Earth's coasts / Bobbie Kalman.

(Looking at earth)
Includes index.
ISBN 978-0-7787-3206-8 (bound).--ISBN 978-0-7787-3216-7 (pbk.)

1. Coasts--Juvenile literature. I. Title. II. Series.

GB453.K34 2008 j551.4'57 C2008-905549-7

Library of Congress Cataloging-in-Publication Data

Kalman, Bobbie.
Earth's coasts / Bobbie Kalman.
p. cm. -- (Looking at earth)
Includes index.
ISBN-13: 978-0-7787-3216-7 (pbk. : alk. paper)
ISBN-10: 0-7787-3216-9 (pbk. : alk. paper)
ISBN-13: 978-0-7787-3206-8 (reinforced library binding : alk. paper)
ISBN-10: 0-7787-3206-1 (reinforced library binding : alk. paper)
1. Coasts--Juvenile literature. I. Title. II. Series.

GB453.K35 2009
551.45'7--dc22

2008035384

Crabtree Publishing Company

www.crabtreebooks.com 1-800-387-7650

Printed in the U.S.A./122016/JF20161111

In Canada: We acknowledge the financial support of the Government of Canada through the Canada Book Fund for our publishing activities.

Published in Canada
Crabtree Publishing
616 Welland Ave.
St. Catharines, ON
L2M 5V6

Published in the United States
Crabtree Publishing
PMB 59051
350 Fifth Avenue, 59th Floor
New York, New York 10118

Published in the United Kingdom
Crabtree Publishing
Maritime House
Basin Road North, Hove
BN41 1WR

Published in Australia
Crabtree Publishing
3 Charles Street
Coburg North
VIC, 3058

Contents

The blue planet

Earth is called the "blue planet" because it is made up mainly of **oceans**, and oceans look blue. Oceans are huge areas of water. There are also big areas of land on Earth. These land areas are called **continents**. Oceans touch the continents at **coasts**. Coasts are the edges of land next to oceans.

What are coastlines?

The map below shows Earth's oceans and continents. There are five oceans and seven continents. The lines between the continents and oceans are **coastlines**. Coastlines are the outlines of coasts.

This coastline is in Australia.

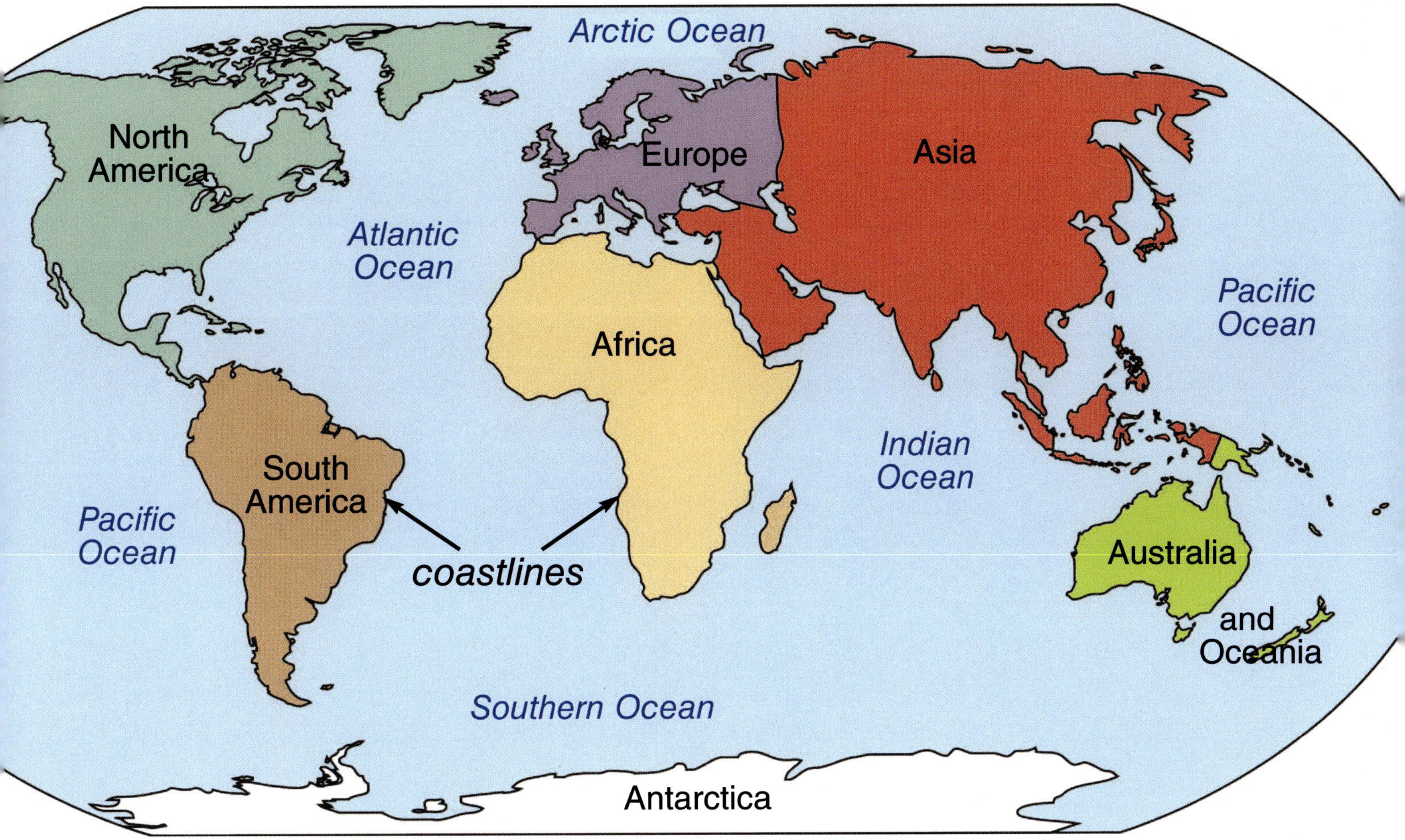

The continents are Asia, Africa, North America, South America, Antarctica, Europe, and Australia and Oceania. What are the names of Earth's oceans? Find them on this map. Which ocean is at the top of Earth? Which ocean is at the bottom? Which is the largest ocean? Did you guess that it is the Pacific Ocean?

Coasts are landforms

A coast is a **landform**. A landform is how land is shaped. Coasts can have very different shapes. In some places, the land at coasts is flat. In other places, the land is tall and steep. Some coasts have big **rock formations**. Rock formations are rocks with unusual shapes. The pictures on these pages show some different kinds of coasts on Earth.

*Some coasts have tall rocks called **cliffs**.*

*Some coasts have flat, sandy **beaches**.*

This rock formation is part of a coast. Which animal does it look like to you?

Some coasts have a lot of ice and snow. This coast is in Antarctica.

Coastal land shapes

The land that makes up coasts can have different shapes. The pictures on these pages show some coastal landforms. They are **island**, **mainland**, **peninsula**, **isthmus**, **headland**, **cape**, **spit**, and **sandbar**.

An island is land that has water all around it. Islands can be small or large.

A peninsula is land that has water almost all around it, but it is connected to a mainland. A mainland is a large land area.

An isthmus is a strip of land that joins two land areas. An isthmus has water on both sides.

A headland is an area of land that juts out into an ocean. It is sometimes called a cape.

A spit is a narrow strip of sand that starts at a coast and sticks out into an ocean.

A sandbar is an area of sand near a coast with shallow water around it.

The ocean at coasts

Coasts have different shapes. The shape of a coast also shapes the water that flows around it. At some coasts, the water follows the curve of the land. At other coasts, the ocean flows inland like a river. Ocean without land near it is called **open ocean**.

*This ocean water is called a **fiord** or **fjord**. A fiord is a type of **inlet**. An inlet is a narrow body of water that flows from a larger body of water. Fiords are found between coasts with tall mountains.*

A **lagoon** is a shallow body of salt water that is separated from ocean water by land or a **coral reef** (see page 22).

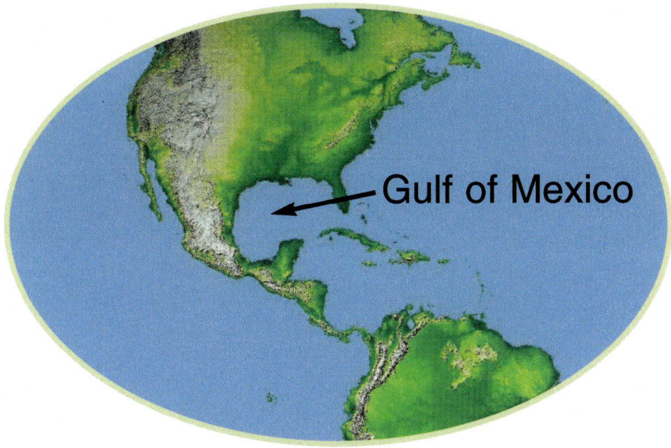

A **gulf** is a big, deep area of ocean that has land almost all around it. This gulf is the Gulf of Mexico. A **strait** is a narrow inlet of water that flows between two oceans.

A **bay** is an area of the ocean where the land curves inward.

A **cove** is a small bay.

A **harbor** is part of a bay that is safe from wind and big waves. A harbor has deep water so boats and ships can sail into it.

Coasts change

Some coasts have cliffs with tall, steep rocks. Ocean waves crash against the cliffs again and again. Over time, some of the rock in the cliffs **erodes**, or wears away. The rock cracks. Water gets into the cracks, and holes form. As more of the cliff falls away, the holes get bigger and become **caves**.

Caves in cliffs

Caves that are made by ocean waves are called **sea caves**. Sea caves can have one or more openings. Ocean water fills some sea caves. The sea cave below has a lot of ocean water. The water in this cave is deep enough for boats.

Breaking away

On narrow cliffs, cave openings reach all the way through the cliff rock. The cave holes become **arches**. An arch is a curved opening. Big waves have cut an arch into this huge cliff.

Tall stacks

After many storms, arches get thinner and weaker. The rock at the top gets very thin, and it falls down. Tall, steep rocks that become separated from cliffs are called **sea stacks**.

This sea stack was once part of the cliff beside it. The top of the arch fell. The sea stack is no longer joined to the cliff.

Stones and sand

After many years, ocean waters break some cliffs into small stones. Later, the stones break down even more and become sand. Sand and stones are found on some beaches. Other beaches have mainly sand. This child is buried in sand at a beach.

Some of the stones at this beach have become sand. It will take many years for the other stones to become sand.

Many **tropical** beaches have fine white sand and shallow water. Tropical beaches are in places that have hot weather all year. They are near the **equator**.

A **dune** is a ridge of sand. Waves carry sand from the ocean, and the wind blows the sand into small hills behind the beach. How can you tell that it is very windy at this beach?

Volcanoes to coasts

Hot lava is pouring into the ocean. Smoke and steam form when the lava reaches the water.

A **volcano** is an opening in the Earth's surface. When a volcano **erupts**, or explodes, smoke, ash, and **lava** shoot out. Lava is red-hot liquid rock. After lava pours out, it dries and gets hard. When lava runs down into an ocean, it cools quickly in the water. The cold lava forms hard black lava rock, called **basalt**. Many coasts are made of basalt.

After many years, ocean water breaks lava rock into black sand. This black-sand beach is in Iceland.

Islands of lava

There are volcanoes under oceans, too. Lava pours out of these volcanoes and forms mountains under water. The tops of the mountains become islands. The Hawaiian Islands are the tops of huge volcanoes. The island on the right is part of a volcano.

Hawaii is part of the United States. The capital of Hawaii is Honolulu. Honolulu is on the island of Oahu.

This map shows seven of Hawaii's islands. The islands were created by volcanoes. Hawaii is a chain of many islands. A chain of islands is called an ***archipelago****.*

Icy coasts

Some coasts are covered in ice and snow for much of the year. These coasts are near the North Pole and the South Pole. The ocean at the North Pole is the Arctic Ocean. The ocean at the South Pole is the Southern Ocean.

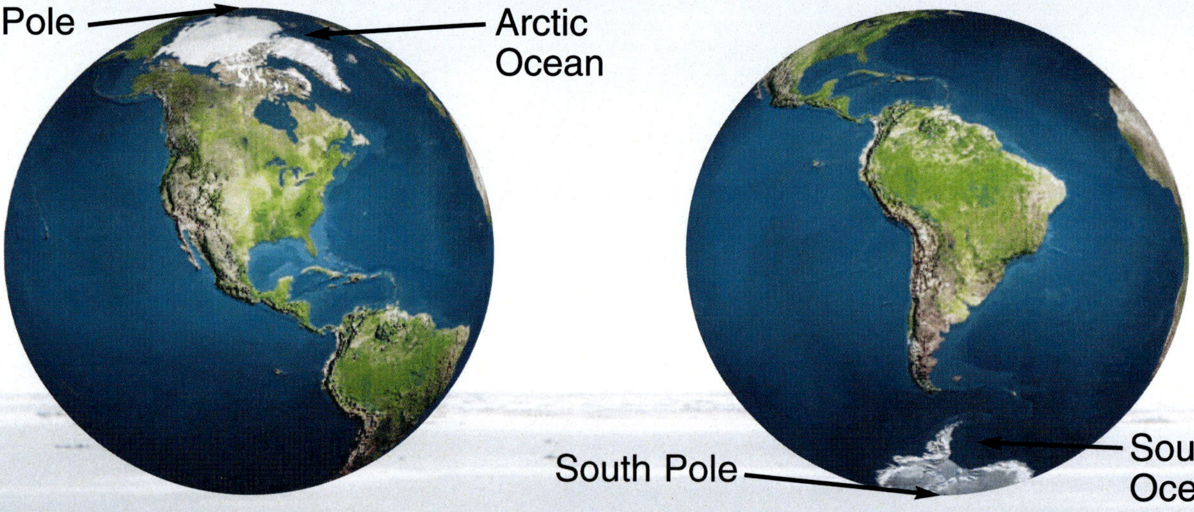

*Polar bears live at the North Pole. This bear is on an **ice floe**. An ice floe is a sheet of floating ice.*

Frozen rivers called glaciers

There are **glaciers** on most continents, but many of Earth's glaciers are near the poles. Glaciers are slow-moving rivers of ice. Glaciers form in areas that have snow in winter and cool weather in summer. The snow turns to ice and begins to flow downwards and outwards. Glaciers cut through rock and change the shape of coasts. This glacier is at a coast in Alaska.

Coast habitats

Habitats are places in nature where plants and animals live. Most ocean plants and animals live in the sunny parts of oceans, where the water is shallow and warm. These areas are near coasts. Coral reefs are ocean habitats that are near coasts. Coral reefs are made up of colorful corals. Corals are animals. Many kinds of fish and other ocean creatures also live in coral reefs.

Sea turtles, corals, many kinds of fish, and other animals live in coral reefs.

At the seashore

Seashores are the edges of sandy or rocky coasts. They are the habitats of many kinds of animals. Crabs crawl along the rocks or beaches. Birds swoop in looking for small ocean animals to eat in **tide pools**. Tide pools are small pools of water that collect between rocks.

Sea stars and sea urchins often get trapped in tide pools such as this one.

River meets coast

Ocean water contains a lot of salt. The water in rivers is **fresh water**. Fresh water does not contain a lot of salt. Rivers flow into bigger bodies of water, such as lakes or oceans. An **estuary** is a body of water at an ocean's coast that has one or more rivers flowing into it. Fresh water meets salt water at an estuary. Water that has both fresh water and salt water is called **brackish** water.

Estuary habitats

This estuary is at the end of the Rio Baru, a river in Costa Rica. The river flows through a **rain forest** and then mixes with salt water at the Pacific Ocean. Many types of rainforest animals depend on this estuary. More than 200 kinds of birds, such as anhingas, visit it to find food and water. Green iguanas also live here. They are everywhere!

anhinga

iguana

People live on coasts

Coasts are habitats for people, too. Many towns and cities are built on coasts. There are four coastal cities shown here. They are Vancouver, Durban, Avalon, and Sydney. Two cities are in North America, one is in Australia, and one is in Africa. Read the clues on the pictures and find the cities on a map or globe.

1. This city is in South Africa. It is on a coast of the Indian Ocean.

2. This city is famous for its opera house. It is in Australia, on the coast of a huge natural harbor, which has the same name. The harbor is part of an estuary near the Pacific Ocean.

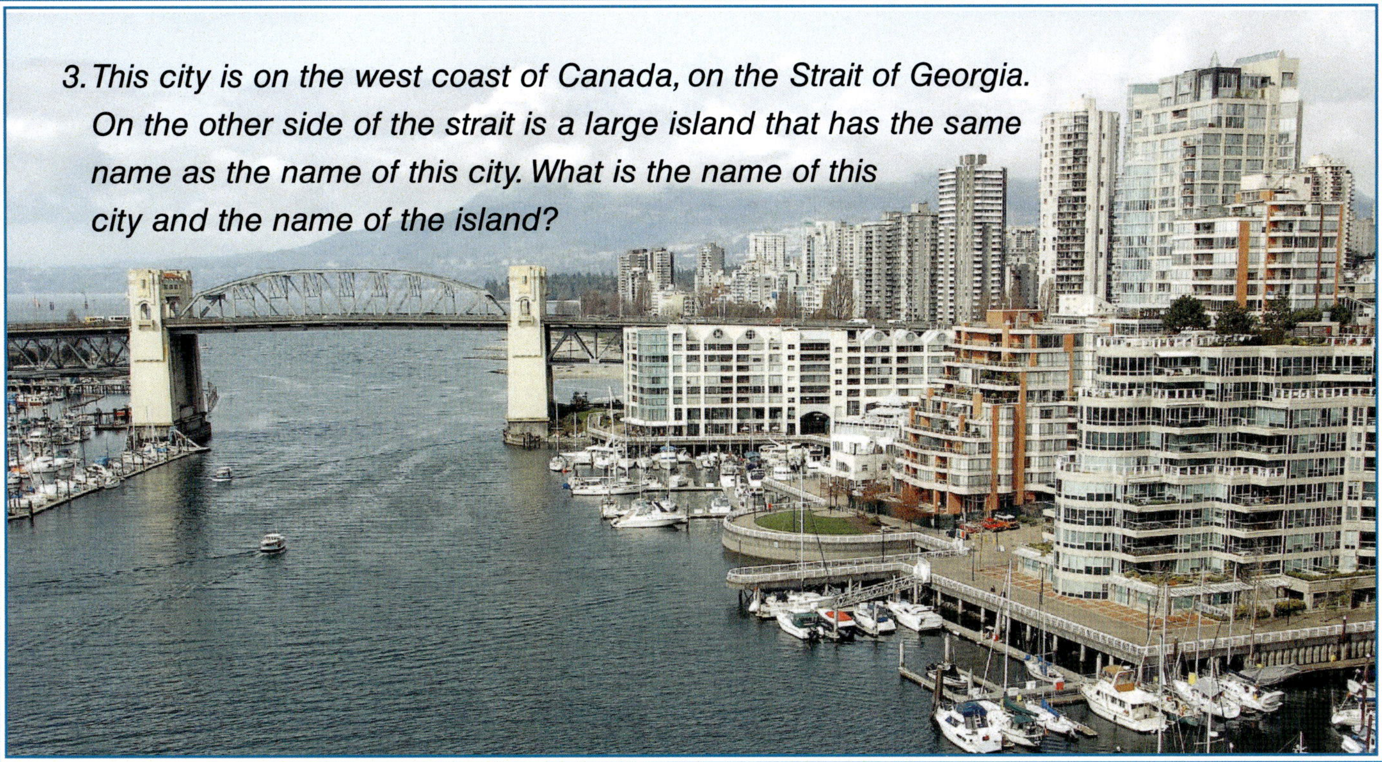

3. This city is on the west coast of Canada, on the Strait of Georgia. On the other side of the strait is a large island that has the same name as the name of this city. What is the name of this city and the name of the island?

4. This small American city is on the coast of an island called Catalina. Catalina is in the Pacific Ocean, near the coast of California.

Answers:

1. Durban 2. Sydney
3. Vancouver and Vancouver Island
4. Avalon

Sun, sea, and sand

Many people travel to coasts for their vacations. At coasts, there are all kinds of fun activities. What would you like to do at a coast?

Would you build a sand castle?

Would you go boogey boarding?

Would you go for a long run?

Other fun activities

There are many ways to enjoy yourself at a coast. You can fly a kite or splash in the waves. Some coasts have beautiful sandy beaches with clear blue water. The water is perfect for snorkeling. What might you see under the sea? Name five kinds of ocean animals you know.

These children are having fun snorkeling in the clear shallow ocean. Have you ever gone snorkeling? What did you see?

I see you!

Coast quiz

You have learned many things about coasts. How much can you remember? The letters in the photographs on these two pages show parts of coasts. Match them to the coast names on the drawing below.

Answers: A-arch; B-cliff; C-sea cave; D-beach; E-lagoon; F-headland; G-bay; H-cove; I-harbor; J-river; K-estuary; L-sea stack; M-peninsula; N-island; O-archipelago

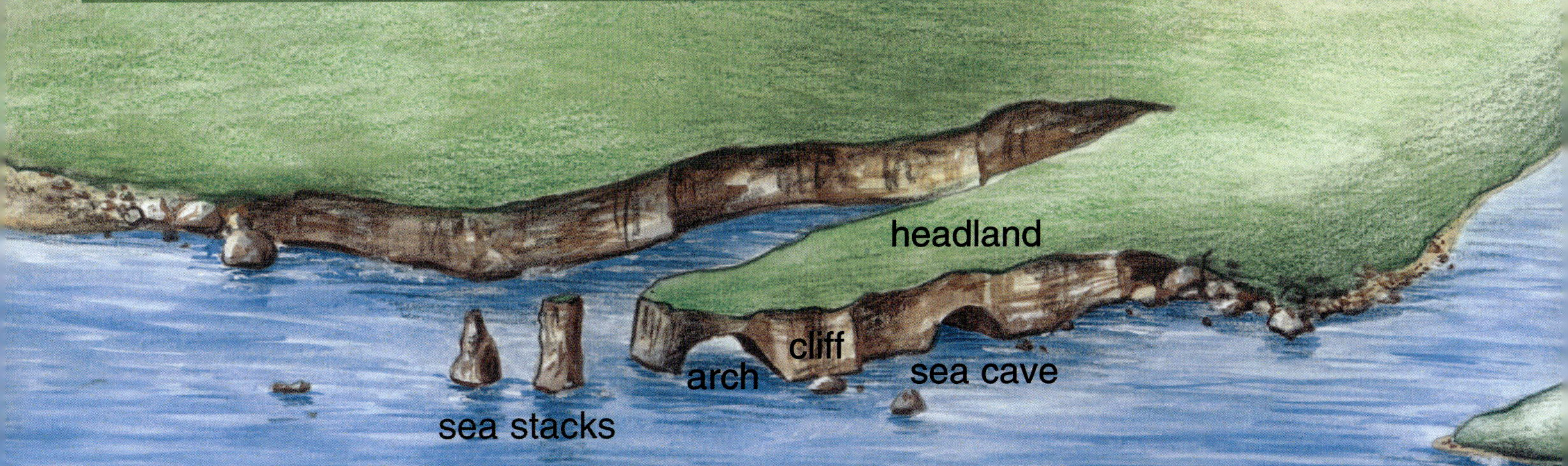

Words to know

Note: Some boldfaced words are defined where they appear in the book.

bay An area of the sea where the land curves inward

beach A sandy coast area that may have small stones

cave A hole that forms under a cliff

cliff A steep area of rock at the edge of an ocean

coral reef An area in the ocean that is made up of live and dead corals

equator An imaginary line around the center of Earth where it is hot all year

harbor A part of a coast where boats are safe from wind and big ocean waves

inlet A narrow body of water that flows inland from an ocean or a lake

lagoon Shallow ocean water that is separated from the open ocean by land or a coral reef

open ocean Ocean water that does not have land near it

peninsula A part of a coast that has water almost all around it

rain forest A forest in a hot area that gets a lot of rain all year

sea stack A tower of rock that was once part of a cliff and has broken away from it

strait A narrow area of water that connects two large areas of water

Index